RAIDERS AT SEA

Lisa Thompson

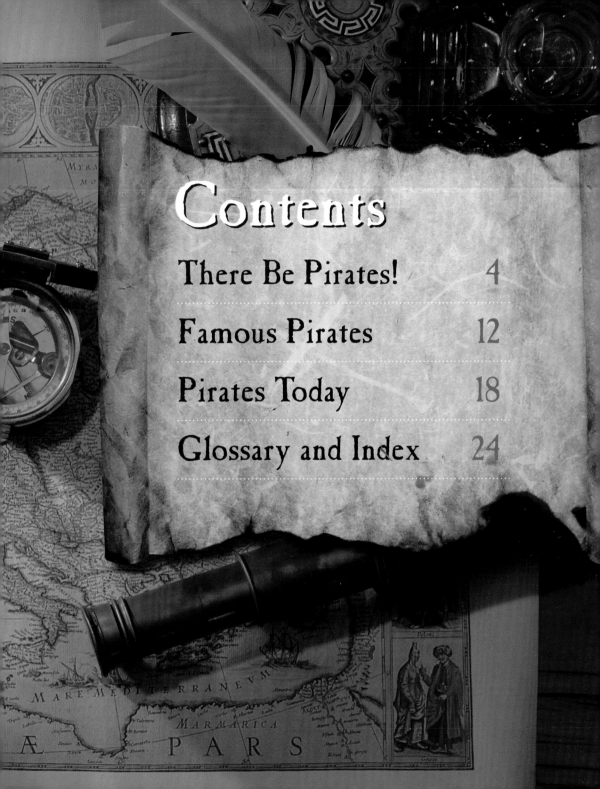

Contents

There Be Pirates!

Pirates are robbers in ships. They attack other ships and ports to steal treasure.

There have been pirates ever since there have been ships. Buccaneers were pirates who sailed the Caribbean Sea, attacking Spanish ships. Corsairs sailed the Mediterranean Sea.

Some pirates stole for the king or queen of their country. Privateers were pirates with a **license** to rob. They were allowed to steal. Some pirates stole only for themselves.

Many pirates were sailors captured from enemy ships.

Today, there are still pirates sailing the seas.

The land around the Caribbean Sea was called The Spanish Main.

All Aboard!

Life at sea was hard.

Pirates spent most of their time on the ship's decks. Treasure, food, water, and weapons were stored below decks.

Pirates kept the outside of their ship — the hull — clean. This made the ship faster. The crew dragged the ship onto a beach to clean it.

 On Black Bart's pirate ship, lights had to be put out at 8 pm.

The pirate captain made rules about how to behave. The crew was punished for breaking the rules.

But pirates often had a party after they robbed a ship.

GUN POWDER

Attack!

Jolly Roger

Pirates tried to surprise their enemies.

The normal pirate flag was the Jolly Roger, but pirates often flew a false flag. When they sailed close to an enemy ship, pirates would show their pirate flag. This surprised the enemy crew who often **surrendered**.

In 1720, Black Bart sailed into a harbor. All his pirate flags were showing. The crews of 22 ships in the harbor quickly surrendered!

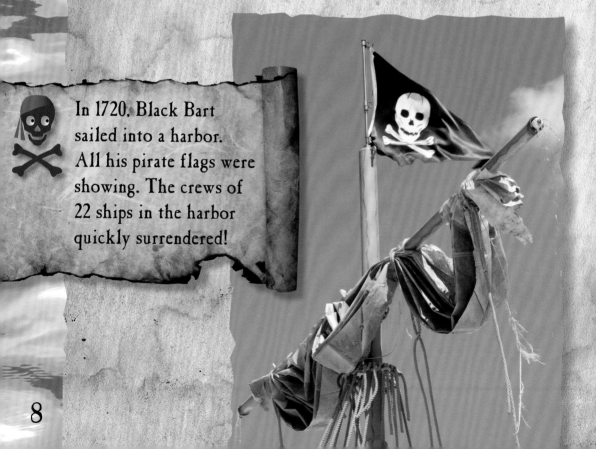

To attack, the pirates threw ropes with hooks at the enemy ship. The hooks caught in the ship's **rigging**. The pirates climbed along the ropes to fight.

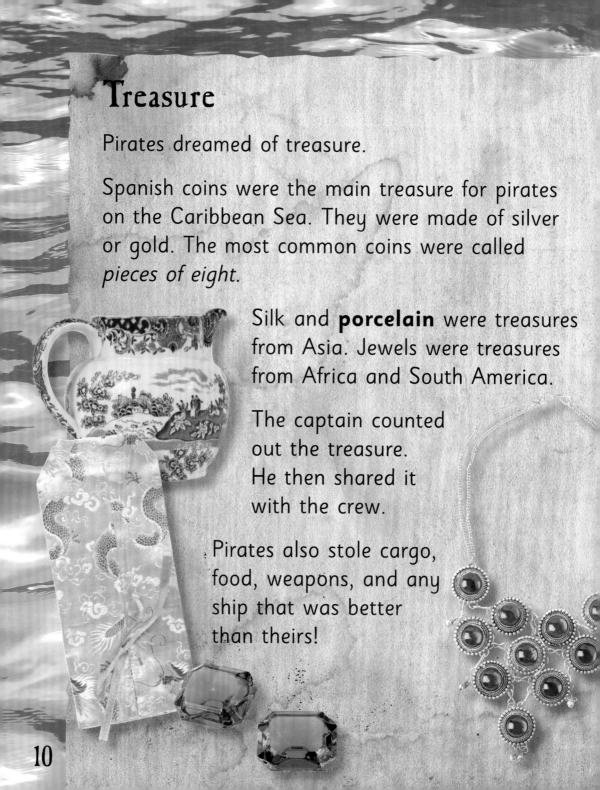

Treasure

Pirates dreamed of treasure.

Spanish coins were the main treasure for pirates on the Caribbean Sea. They were made of silver or gold. The most common coins were called *pieces of eight*.

Silk and **porcelain** were treasures from Asia. Jewels were treasures from Africa and South America.

The captain counted out the treasure. He then shared it with the crew.

Pirates also stole cargo, food, weapons, and any ship that was better than theirs!

Spanish Coins

name of coin	it was worth	it was made of
real	1 real	silver
piece of eight	8 reales	silver
escudo	16 reales	gold
doubloon	128 reales	gold

Most pirates did not bury their treasure. They spent it!

Famous Pirates

Captain Kidd

Captain Kidd was not always a pirate. It was once his job to catch pirates.

In 1698, Captain Kidd attacked a ship near India. The *Quedagh Merchant* was loaded with gold, silver, jewels, sugar, and guns. Captain Kidd kept the ship. He gave it a new name — *Adventure Prize*.

Finally, he was arrested and hanged. People are still looking for Captain Kidd's buried treasure.

Blackbeard

Blackbeard's real name was Edward Teach.
His nickname came from his long, braided,
black beard.

During battle, Blackbeard hid burning **fuses**
under his hat. The smoke from the fuses
made him look dangerous. He captured
40 ships in two years.

Mary Read

Mary Read often dressed as a man. One day, a ship she was on was captured by pirates. The pirate captain let Mary become a pirate.

Mary became best friends with the captain's girlfriend, Anne Bonny.

Anne Bonny

Anne Bonny was also called Toothless Annie. She dressed and fought like other pirates.

When their ship was attacked, Anne and Mary fought together. The rest of the crew stayed below decks!

Pirates thought it was unlucky to start a voyage on a Friday.

Captain Hook

Captain Hook is in the story *Peter Pan*. He has a hook instead of his right hand. His hand was cut off by Peter Pan and eaten by a crocodile.

The crocodile follows Hook around, waiting for another bite.

Long John Silver

Long John Silver is in the story *Treasure Island*. He has only one leg. A parrot named Captain Flint sits on his shoulder.

Long John Silver searches for treasure hidden by a pirate called Billy Bones.

Pirates Today

Modern pirates attack ships and fishing boats.

They often use small, fast speedboats. They attack when large ships slow down in narrow waters. Sometimes, the pirates don't want cargo. They want the ship's crew. They take their belongings and kidnap them.

This is a modern pirate ship.

Modern pirates can take over a large cargo ship because the ship only has a small crew.

Modern pirates often disguise their ships to look like fishing boats or cargo ships.

Modern pirates often pretend to be fishermen.

Where Are Pirates Now?

Most pirate attacks are near Indonesia.

Many attacks occur in the narrow Strait of Malacca. This is the main way for ships to travel between the Indian Ocean and the Pacific Ocean. More than 50,000 ships use it every year.

The port of Chittagong in Bangladesh is the most dangerous in the world. Pirates attack ships that **moor** near the port.

Pirates also rob ships around Africa. In Nigeria, they have attacked ships from canoes.

Pirates may climb ropes and anchor chains.

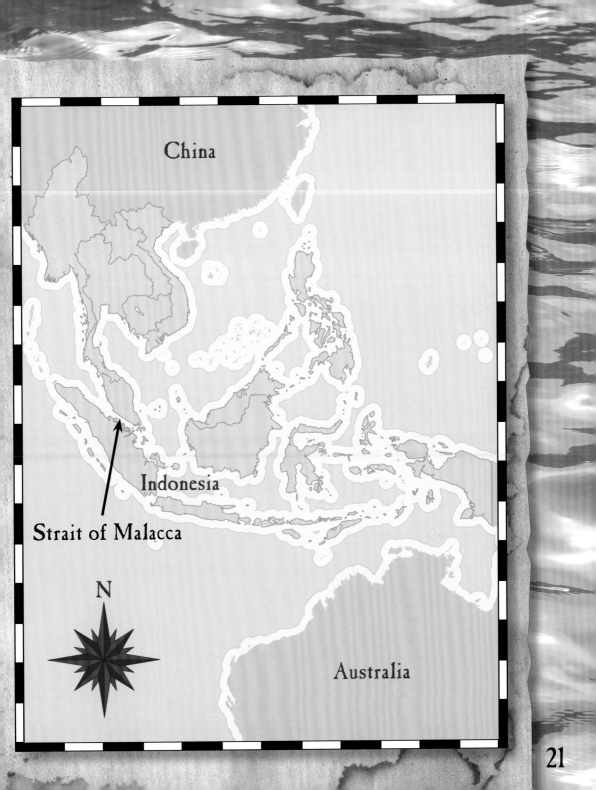

China

Indonesia

Strait of Malacca

N

Australia

Modern Pirate Attacks

RED SEA PIRATES

March 2007

Pirates fired guns at a ship in the Red Sea. A navy ship came to help. The pirates were captured.

SUPERTANKER ATTACKED

March 2003

Pirates attacked a supertanker in the Strait of Malacca. They did not steal cargo or hurt the crew. The pirates wanted to learn how to steer the ship.

Ships Collide

Pirates attacked an oil tanker. They threw the crew overboard. There was no one to steer the tanker. The pirates left the ship sailing at full speed.

Glossary

fuse a string used to set off a bomb or firecracker

license a document which gives permission to do something

moor to tie up a boat

porcelain cups and plates made of clay

rigging the ropes and chains on a ship's masts

surrender to stop fighting and admit defeat

Index